Kailin, Liam &
Keira

W is for Woof
A Dog Alphabet

Happy Valentines
Day 2009

Love,
Amy, Jacob
Greg

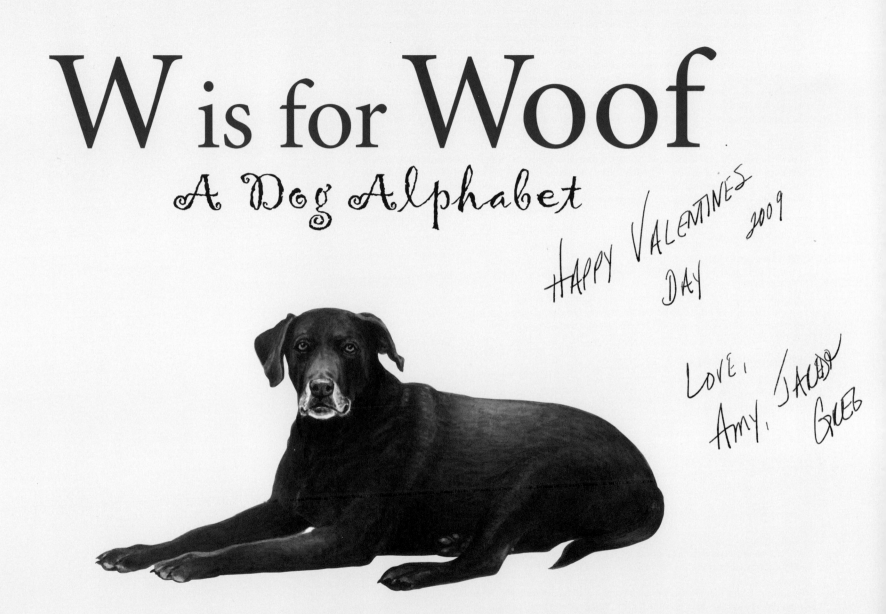

Written by Ruth Strother and Illustrated by Gijsbert van Frankenhuyzen

Author's acknowledgments

I would like to thank Cindy Planchak and Pam Pedaline for lending me their teacher's eye. And I'm indebted to Paula Terifaj, DVM, for her knowledge and insights into the world of dogs.

Illustrator's acknowledgments

There are as many thank-you's for this book as there are letters in the alphabet. My thanks and appreciation go out to all the dogs and their owners/trainers for their patience, generosity, enthusiasm and hard work in making this book come to life. For those dogs and owners who didn't make it into the book, (and you know who you are) thank you, too, for your eagerness to help out. So without further ado, and in no particular order, thank you to: all the folks and their dogs from the Midland A.K.C. Dog Show; Ben Perez & Bella; Dwight Reed from the Book Store in Frankfort; Dr. David Batch, John French, and the staff of the Abrams Planetarium; Lise and Pete Dibert & Tilly; Courtney Adams & Lily of Zeeb's Pet Health Center; Mary Wrigley & Tag Along and Maeve; Officer Kay Van Ells & K-9 Coby; Annie Fanta & Kobe; Johanna Williams & Daisy; LaVone Forsman & her twelve lab pups with Alec Webb and Ryan Weiss; Connie Friedly & Sherlock; Beri Bouwman & Rose and Libby; Officer Joaquin Guerrero & K-9 Rookie; Cindy Van Pelt, the counselor of Perry Elementary School and Deanna Vandemark & Elle; McKain Williams, Dr. Beth Burmeister D.V.M. and Dr. Kevin Harris D.V.M. & Bella of the Haslett Animal Hospital; Rachelle Kniffen, Tom Hill & Flynn from the Rochester Leader Dogs for the Blind; Rachel and Kelvin Potter & their dogs P.D. and Letty; to all the folks from the Williamston Agility Dog Show; and finally to Rebecca Yonker, Linda Gates, and the entire staff of the Capital Area Humane Society and all the dogs and puppies awaiting new homes.

Sleeping Bear Press™

310 North Main Street, Suite 300
Chelsea, MI 48118
www.sleepingbearpress.com

© 2008 Sleeping Bear Press is an imprint of Gale, a part of Cengage Learning.

Printed and bound in China.

10 9 8 7 6 5 4 3 2 1

Library of Congress Cataloging-in-Publication Data

Strother, Ruth.
W is for woof : a dog alphabet / written by Ruth Strother ;
illustrated by Gijsbert van Frankenhuyzen. — 1st ed.
p. cm.
Summary: "Using the alphabet format to learn about dog behavior, domestication, grooming, K-9 police dogs, and much more. Simple poetry for each topic is paired with detail-filled expository text. Realistic illustrations complement the text"—
Provided by publisher.
ISBN 978-1-58536-343-8
1. Dogs—Juvenile literature. 2. English language—Alphabet—Juvenile literature. I. Frankenhuyzen, Gijsbert van, ill. II. Title.
SF426.5.S78 2008
636.7—dc22   2007026085

To Andy and Stephanie

RUTH

To Rookie

GIJSBERT

A a

A is for American Kennel Club

Big dogs, small dogs; ears pricked, tails curled,
breeds from all around the world
stay true and perfect as can be,
under the watchful eye of the AKC.

All dog breeds belong to the same species: *Canis familiaris*. Breeds were first developed accidentally because people wanted to duplicate their dogs' best traits. They mated their most skilled hunting dogs, for example, or their cutest companion dogs. A new breed was created when the favored traits showed up in puppies generation after generation.

Many kennel clubs, such as the American Kennel Club (AKC), act as registries that standardize and uphold the traits of each breed. These standards include such details as height, weight, coat color and texture, head shape, and temperament. Clubs host shows, among other activities, to determine the best example of each breed. The most famous of these shows is the annual Westminster Kennel Club Dog Show.

From the time the AKC and other dog clubs began to specify breed standards, breeders have been working to meet those standards to perfection.

AMERICAN KENNEL CLUB

AKC

FOUNDED 1884

TM

FIRST PRIZE

★ ★ ★ ★

B is for Behavior

Dogs jump and bow and bark and mark
and rest quietly at your feet.
You need to read their body language
'cause dogs don't really speak.

Bow Wow!

Dogs are social animals. Left on their own, they form family-like units that we call packs. When no other dogs are around, a dog will form a pack with his human family—after all, we're social animals, too.

Dogs have specific behaviors and physical cues to help them live together harmoniously. The leader of the pack, also called the top dog, the dominant dog, or the alpha dog, holds himself tall and proud. Other dogs recognize his body language and act submissively, staying lower than the alpha dog. While the alpha dog's tail is held straight out, the submissive dog's tail is held down. While the alpha dog's ears are pricked up, the submissive dog's ears are held back and laid flat on the head.

A lot of behavior problems we see are merely misplaced natural pack behaviors. Jumping on people, for instance, stems from puppies jumping up on their mother and licking her lips. That's how they get her to regurgitate food for their dining pleasure. Understanding the source of an unwanted behavior is key to finding a solution to the problem.

Bb

C is for Constellations

Faraway stars sparkle light and bright,
form into shapes in the long dark night.
Big Dog, Little Dog, Hunting Dogs, all
can be seen in the sky before the moon falls.

Constellations are patterns of stars that form shapes in the night sky. These connect-the-dots pictures were imagined by ancient peoples to identify one star from another. Myths were fashioned around each constellation to explain how it came to be. These stories are associated with the constellations to this day.

Dogs are found in three of the eighty-eight constellations. Canes Venatici shows two greyhounds chasing a bear around the North Pole with Boötes, the Bear Driver, who has them on a leash. Canis Major (the Great Dog) and Canis Minor (the Lesser Dog) are Orion's hunting companions.

Sirius (the Dog Star) is part of Canis Major. It's the brightest star in the sky. In late July, it rises and sets with the sun. Ancient peoples thought that the Dog Star added to the sun's heat, so the Romans named this scorching time of year Dog Days. That's how we get the phrase "the dog days of summer."

D d

D is for Domestication

Domestication is adaptation
to life with human association.
Living together is the sensation,
and in the end, it's a great relation.

The domestication of animals has greatly improved life for humans. One of the biggest success stories of domestication is that of the dog from the wolf. It helped that the social structure of the wolf pack and the human family were much alike.

Some scientists believe that the domestication of the dog occurred a distant 40,000 to 135,000 years ago. The more popular theory dates domestication to 13,000 to 17,000 years ago. Wolves, scientists think, were attracted to discarded food around villages. Those who were not so afraid of people ate more of the food. They were more likely to survive and produce ever bolder and friendlier puppies. In time, the wolves' guarding and hunting skills were noticed by the villagers. People worked out ways to use those skills to their benefit. Wolf and human interaction became closer and more comfortable. Eventually, wolf adaptations led to domestication and to a new species—the dog.

Dogs are famous for their acute sense of smell, but their other senses are important as well. They can hear sounds from farther away and at higher and lower ranges than we can. While wolves have erect ears, their pups' ears are floppy. Today's floppy-eared breeds were developed to be puppy-wolf cute. Dogs with erect ears have an advantage, though, because their ears cup and amplify sounds. They can also move one ear at a time to help pinpoint what they're hearing.

Although dogs don't see as well as we do, their night and peripheral vision are better than ours. Moving objects easily catch their attention, which helped their wild ancestors while on the hunt. Their world isn't as colorful as ours, though. Dogs see shades of gray and toned-down greens and reds. But no matter; it's the visual cues that are important in dog society. Tail and ear position, belly-up submission, and inviting play bow are all essential communications.

E e

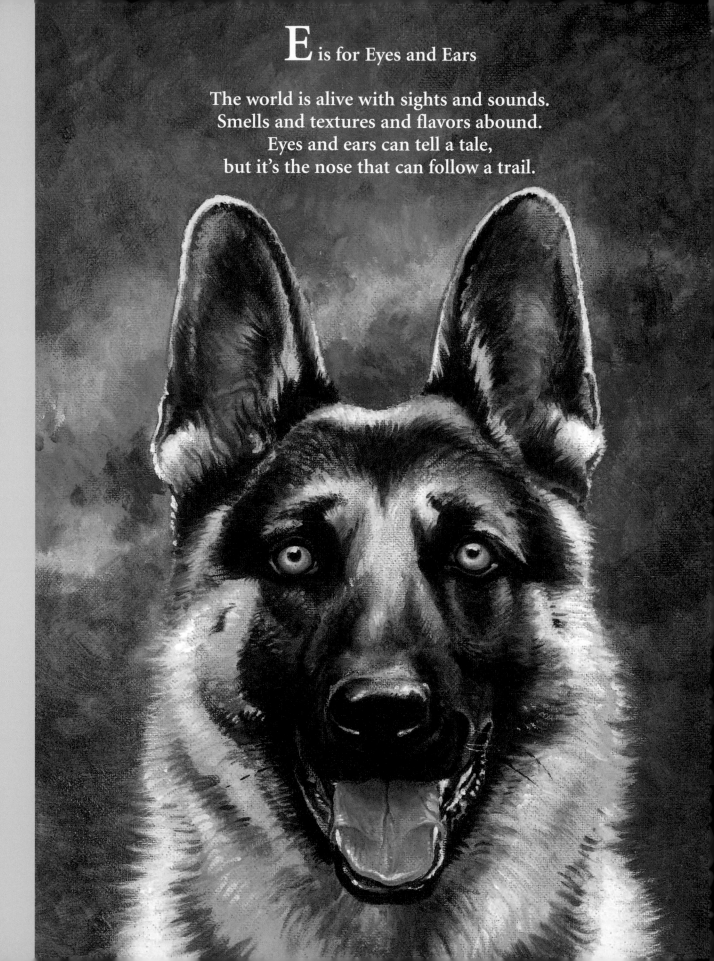

E is for Eyes and Ears

The world is alive with sights and sounds.
Smells and textures and flavors abound.
Eyes and ears can tell a tale,
but it's the nose that can follow a trail.

Ff

F is for Fun

There's nothing better to a dog
than having something fun to do.
A race, a game, a zippy jog
and your dog will say thank you!

Many breeds were developed to perform a specific job for people. Today's dogs, however, are not often called to task, yet they still have their inbred urges egging them on and often getting them into mischief. Fortunately a variety of fun activities have been designed to take advantage of these natural urges. Many are best suited to certain breeds, but any breed, including mixed breeds in many cases, are generally welcomed.

Agility is among the organized activities available to dogs. Herding breeds especially excel at this timed obstacle course. Frisbee, also called canine disc, is a sport well suited to herding and gun dogs. Terriers can compete in earthdog trials; field trials and hunt tests are custom made for gun dogs and hounds. The northern breeds enjoy sledding and skijoring—instead of sleds, mushers compete on skis with a team of one to three dogs. Flyball is a relay race great for any dog with a competitive spirit.

Many more activities can be found to keep a dog busy and satisfied. Some even have junior versions in which kids younger than eighteen can participate. But don't forget you can always have fun with your dog just playing fetch in your fenced-in backyard!

G is for Grooming

Brush out the mats, comb out the fleas—
shampoo and conditioner, if you please.
Grooming your dog keeps her healthy and clean.
Put a bow in her fur and she may even preen.

Dog grooming has a history that dates back thousands of years. Poodlelike dogs of long ago sported a style similar to the modern day lion clip. Lions symbolized strength and power. People wanted those qualities in their dogs. Fishermen welcomed the hairdo because it helped these water retrievers swim better. A poodle's fur gets heavy when wet, so areas were shaved to help keep the dogs afloat. The lionlike mane and puffy fur around the chest and ankles kept them warm.

Professional grooming is still done for style and utility today. But grooming is important to every dog's health. Daily brushing and periodic shampooing keep a dog's skin healthy and fur shiny. You also get the chance to check for fleas, ticks, and lumps on your dog's body. Cleaning ears helps prevent infections, and clipping nails keeps them from growing too long. Brushing your dog's teeth is important to prevent gum disease— and to get rid of that doggy breath!

You could have your dog groomed professionally. Do it at home, though, and you get the added benefit of strengthening the bond between you and your dog.

Gg

H is for Herding

Bring them together, lickety-split.
      Don't miss a one is the herding dog's trick.
They gather the herd from the pasture with skill
    and guide them back home, the dogs know the drill.

Hh

Centuries ago, cattle and sheep grazed across acres of unfriendly land. It would take hours, days even, for ranchers to gather and drive home their livestock. They needed help. Dogs with their built-in herding instincts were called into service.

Herding breeds were developed in various countries. Each breed was shaped to meet the specific demands of local terrain and livestock. Cattle dogs, for instance, herd by nipping at the livestock's feet. Sheepdogs take a predatory stance. They stay low to the ground, controlling their flock with a piercing stare.

Ranchers and their herding dogs seem to be of one mind when they work. Without question or hesitation, dogs respond to a rancher's cues. But when working at a distance, herding dogs think and solve problems for themselves.

Today there are few opportunities to ranch. Much of the herding done now is seen in competitions, and many of the entrants are city folk. Needless to say, herding dogs are extremely active and smart. Have one as a pet and you better line up a slew of activities to keep him busy!

The Iditarod trail was first used to deliver mail and supplies from coastal Alaska to the interior. Dogsled was the best way to travel through the freezing, windy, and snowy landscape. When an epidemic hit the children of Nome in 1925, mushers grabbed their dogsleds and rushed across the Iditarod trail with lifesaving medicine.

Today the Iditarod is a 1,150-mile race honoring the history of the trail. Every year on the first weekend in March, mushers with teams of twelve to sixteen dogs, mostly huskies, line up in Anchorage to start the race. Nine to seventeen days later, the teams straggle into Nome. A shorter race, the Junior Iditarod, is held the previous week for fourteen- to seventeen-year-old mushers.

You don't have to race in the Iditarod to mush, though. Many people and dogs enjoy dogsledding as a hobby.

Ii

I is for Iditarod

In the stark white cold the race is on,
The Last Great Race on Earth.
Through ice and snow the dog teams run,
pulling for all they're worth.
Mush!

J j

J is for Junior Showmanship

Enter the ring tall and proud,
    your dog trotting by your side.
In this show kids are allowed,
    they're the ones the judges eye.

Dog clubs hold a variety of events designed to promote breed standards and abilities. Agility, field trials, tracking, and obedience are just a few of the options. The most familiar of the events is the dog show, where conformation is judged. Conformation focuses on the physical structure, or form, of a dog and how it matches the breed standard.

Most clubs have junior versions of competition for kids. Junior Showmanship is a conformation competition. Instead of evaluating the dogs, though, judges evaluate the handlers. Junior handlers are judged on their ability to show their dogs. Some clubs also evaluate the handlers' knowledge of dogs and the breed they are showing.

German and Belgian police were the first officers on record to work with dogs. That was in the late 1800s. Today the breeds most used in police work still come from those countries. They include the Belgian Malinois, German shepherd, and rottweiler.

Many think of police dogs as fierce, frightening animals. In reality they are highly trained dogs whose work is nothing more to them than a great game of fetch or tug. Tracking dogs, usually bloodhounds, find missing people or bad guys in hiding. Detection dogs find bombs and other illegal substances. Patrol dogs are trained to chase and catch suspects by biting onto an arm or a leg. They release the suspect as soon as their police handler tells them to. When successful, a police dog's reward is time with a favorite toy or game.

K-9 police and their human partners work and live side by side, day and night. They depend on each other during life or death situations and share a very close bond. When the dogs retire, they become their partners' full-time pets.

K is for K-9 Police Dogs

Side by side police dogs work
with their human partner coppers.
The K-9s go where dangers lurk.
The weapons used? They use their choppers.

L₁

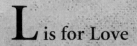

L is for Love

The wag of a tail and the puppy-dog eyes
show love and devotion through years gone by.
Forever friends, your dog and you.
You can count on this love to always be true.

It's no accident that dogs are described as "man's best friend." They are hardwired with the wolf pack's social instinct. Members of a pack help each other with the chores of life such as hunting and caring for pups. Each wolf relies on the rest of the pack for survival; each wolf cares about the others' well-being. This empathy strengthens the bonds and the sense of loyalty among pack members.

Throughout the domestication process, loyalty and empathy between dogs and people grew. Accounts of canine heroism go back thousands of years, and special bonds between famous people and their dogs can be found in our history books. It's true no one can really get into a dog's mind. But there is no denying that dogs have feelings of joy and grief, likes and dislikes. Some may question whether dogs can "love," but emotions that have been attributed to dogs such as devotion and selflessness come awfully close.

Many people prefer mixed-breed dogs. They claim that mixed breeds, also called mutts, random-breds, mongrels, and curs, are healthier and lack the physical limitations that plague some purebred dogs.

On the other hand, a purebred's size, coat style, and temperament are much more predictable than those of mixed breeds. When choosing a dog, it's helpful to know if the breed tends to be active or sedentary; stubborn or agreeable.

Lately, "designer dogs" have been the rage. Breeders mate two breeds with specific characteristics. The result is a hybrid that they claim has the best qualities from each breed. You've probably heard of cockapoos (part cocker spaniel, part poodle) and Labradoodles (part Labrador retriever, part standard poodle). Many in the dog fancy, however, see designer dogs as, well, expensive mutts.

M is for Mixed Breeds

A poodle, Lab, or Afghan hound
may have a pedigree.
But mixed breed dogs are all around.
Which one is right for me?

N is for New Dog

The new dog is coming home today.
Household dangers are all stored away.
Food and bed and collar and leash
are at the ready—it's time to teach!

Bringing a new dog into your family is an important decision. Before you cuddle that cute Saint Bernard puppy or toss a ball for that fun-loving Lab, be sure you know exactly what you want in a dog. That Saint Bernard puppy may be cute, but if you live in a tiny apartment or hate having hair and drool all over the place, this breed is not right for you.

Before bringing your new puppy or dog home, you need to puppy-proof your house. Get down on your hands and knees for a dog's-eye view. Have an adult remove or secure any dangerous items. These include electrical wires, poisonous plants, and household chemicals. Remove all breakables from tabletops and put your toys away! Many kid toys are a lot like dog toys, and dogs usually can't tell the difference.

Some trainers recommend taking your new dog for a walk before bringing him home. This gives you a chance to get to know each other and establish yourself as the leader. If you already have a dog, introduce the two away from the home to avoid any territorial scuffles.

O is for Obedience

A dog who sits, and comes, and stays,
and, overall, one who obeys,
is calm and happy and carefree
because she knows how she must be.

A well-trained dog is a happy dog. She doesn't have to worry about whether she is being good or bad. She knows the rules.

Most trainers use some form of positive reinforcement, like praise or a favorite treat. Rewarding good behavior just makes sense. The trick is timing.

To dogs, any praise or discipline relates to what they are doing at that moment. If we're not quick enough, the dog will be doing something else by the time we're ready with the reward. All too often we end up rewarding the wrong behavior. Some people use clickers to time their rewards more accurately. Dogs are taught to associate the sound of a click with a reward. Each click lets the dog know she's acting correctly at that moment.

Dogs who have learned the basic commands sit, down, stay, and come are well behaved and fun to be with. The AKC even offers the Canine Good Citizen certificate to recognize well-mannered companion dogs. One of the best parts about training a dog, though, is that it makes your friendship stronger.

Oo

P p

Falling in love with a puppy is easy. Puppies are cute, funny, and cuddly. They're also energy-filled fur balls who might chew your prized toys or go potty on your bedroom rug. Time and patience is needed to raise the ideal dog. Understanding your puppy's growing-up stages is the first step to directing energy and avoiding problem behavior.

Most puppies are ready to leave their canine family for a new home when they are about eight weeks old. The problem is that they go through a fear stage at about that time as well. Whatever you do, don't pet your puppy and coo, "it's okay," when he is afraid. That's rewarding the fearful behavior. Instead act happy and upbeat so your puppy will think *Hey, this isn't so bad—it's kind of fun!* Puppies need plenty of positive experiences to help them through this stage.

As they continue to grow, puppies need to be exposed to all sorts of new situations and objects. You can begin this socialization right away—even if the puppy is only eight weeks old. Have your puppy walk on different surfaces such as tile, carpet, concrete, and grass. Run the vacuum cleaner, bang pots, and have someone ring the doorbell. Becoming familiar with the variety of life helps build a puppy's confidence.

At ten weeks or so, most puppies are ready for puppy kindergarten. And in a few weeks, puppies will start to understand social structure, so this is a good time to establish yourself as the leader of your "pack." Puppies will also start getting their adult teeth soon, so chewing will likely become their favorite pastime. Be sure you have one or two of your puppy's most favored chew toys, and direct him to them whenever you catch him chewing on an off-limits item.

Puppies go through another fear stage when they are around four months old. Socialization is especially important during this stage. Puppies should be exposed to other dogs and other animals, children, shopping centers, cars, and loud noises. The more variety the better!

At six months, the teenage stage begins. Puppies start to challenge people's position as top dog. Continued training and patience come in handy. The time to spay or neuter a puppy, if it hasn't already been done, is when a puppy is six months old.

While going through the stages of growing up, puppies also need to learn how to live in a house. That means housetraining. No matter which method is used, prevention of accidents is the key to success. (Never rub a puppy's nose in his mess—it's just cruel and the pup doesn't learn anything.) If you consistently reward good behavior and always let your dog out to go potty after eating, sleeping, and playing, housetraining will be a snap.

P is for Puppies

Playful puppies bound and nip.
They like to chew, they often yip.
But when they settle down to rest,
even the wild ones are the best.

The dog's sense of smell is legendary. With 200 million or so olfactory receptors (we humans have a mere 40 million), dogs are known to be world-class sniffers. The dog's wet nose traps scents better than if it were dry, and the mucous membrane is folded to increase the surface area for absorbing those scents. It's no wonder dogs are called upon to sniff out people and illegal drugs.

Some dogs are especially talented sniffers. Trailing and tracking dogs, such as bloodhounds, keep their noses to the ground. Their long, pendulous ears drag and sweep odors toward the nose. Their facial folds and loose, moist lips help trap the scent particles. Air-scenting dogs pick up traces of scent that drift in the air. Weather conditions can affect the dog's success. But when searching for people trapped in collapsed buildings or those who have drowned, air scenting is the way to go.

Q is for Quest

Nose in the air or to the ground
the dog is on a quest
to chase a scent until it's found
and she does it all with zest.
Sniff, sniff.

R r

To us, search and rescue (SAR) dogs are canine heroes. But to the dogs, search and rescue is just a fun game of hide and seek. SAR is serious business though. We're probably most familiar with disaster SAR dogs. The Oklahoma City bombing in 1995 and the September 11, 2001, World Trade Center attacks brought these amazing dogs to the forefront. Other types of SAR dogs include wilderness rescue dogs, avalanche dogs, and water search and recovery dogs. Of course the dogs don't work all by themselves. They live, train, and work with a handler.

Dog and handler must have a close relationship and work well together. When a SAR dog finds a victim, he gives an alert such as digging, barking, or lying down. The alert may vary depending on whether the victim is alive or dead. It's up to the handler to recognize and interpret the alert. It's also the handler who always rewards the dog after a victim is found. The reward is what motivates SAR dogs—it's the reason they do their job so well. For most dogs, the reward comes in the form of a favorite toy, a game of tug, or some other favorite goody.

All SAR dogs rely on their sense of smell. Wilderness rescue dogs search by air scent or by trailing. Searchers use air-scenting dogs if they're unable to pinpoint the area in which the person was lost. With their noses to the ground, trailing dogs are usually used to track a person who has wandered off on foot.

Avalanche dogs are trained to find people under many feet of snow. They have to act quickly since people survive only a short time when buried by a snowslide. Medium-sized dogs with heavy double coats are most often used as avalanche dogs. The double coat keeps them warm, and the size allows people to load them onto helicopters.

Water search and recovery is a bit different from the other types of SAR. This is a recovery mission, not a rescue mission—the victim has drowned. The dog can detect human scent because it rises to the water's surface and is picked up by the wind. Water recovery dogs are usually trained in both air scenting and trailing. They work from shore, a boat, or in the water.

In most cases, these dog-human rescue teams are certified volunteers. They commit time and money—sometimes thousands of dollars a year—to stay in top form so they are ready when they are called to service. They are true heroes.

R is for Rescue Dogs

Dogs to the rescue! They answer the call
and can find us in any disaster.
These dogs are heroes, one and all.
Saving lives is what they have mastered.

Shelters and rescue groups find homes for stray animals. Dogs with identification such as a tag, a registered tattooed number, or a registered microchip can be reunited with their families. The others stay at the shelter and hope for a new home. Sadly, there is not enough room to house all the unwanted pets. Over five million cats and dogs are destroyed each year. Each one of them could have been a loving pet if given the chance.

There is hope. The number one weapon against pet overpopulation is spaying and neutering. These are safe procedures that do not alter a pet's temperament or energy level. They just keep animals from reproducing. Many shelter and rescue groups spay or neuter every dog who comes through their doors. It's that important.

S is for Strays and Shelters

Some dogs are lucky, they have loving homes.
Others have nowhere to go so they roam.
Shelters step in with wide-open arms,
keeping these rovers safe from harm.

S s

T

t

T is for Therapy Dogs

Dogs give us joy; they let us hope.
They often give us ways to cope.
A pat, a tail wag, head on lap,
dogs make us feel good in a snap.

Therapy dogs work in a variety of roles. Those involved in animal-assisted activities entertain and offer companionship to patients. Connecting with a dog can lead people out of loneliness and sadness. Animal-assisted therapy dogs help people who are going through physical therapy. Brushing or walking a dog can help build strength and muscle control.

Some schools and libraries sponsor literacy programs that include reading therapy dogs. Calm, attentive, and companionable, these dogs lend a willing ear to kids for reading practice. The kids don't have to worry about anyone judging them, and they have fun reading to the dog.

Therapy dogs go through a training program to be certified. They must love people and cannot be at all aggressive. People involved with animal-assisted therapy must be dedicated and have the time to get involved. Studies continually show that therapy dogs do help people heal and improve their skills.

City dogs and their owners face some challenges. Space is limited in apartments and exercise areas may be hard to find. A barking dog won't be tolerated and is better suited to country or suburban life. But some breeds are just fine with city living.

Low-energy, small to medium-sized dogs are good urban-living candidates. Breeds like dachshunds, shih tzus, and pugs don't need much exercise as long as they aren't overweight. But even some larger, more active dogs can do well in the city.

Dog walkers and doggy day cares are becoming more available in urban areas. Those dogs who are left alone for the whole day can get some relief and exercise from a dog walker. To meet a dog's social and physical needs, doggy day cares are the way to go. They offer a playground-like atmosphere, where dogs can romp with other dogs.

With a bit of planning and good breed choice, dogs can be a happy part of urban life.

U is for Urban Dogs

The city made of concrete,
          with grass just here and there,
may not seem like a dog's beat,
          but some breeds just don't care.

A dog's health depends on good medical care and a nutritious diet. Your veterinarian can help with both.

After a puppy gets all of his booster shots, a once-a-year visit to the vet is recommended. This is a good time for you to ask questions or voice any concerns you have about your dog. The checkup includes an examination of the dog's ears, eyes, nose, mouth, heart, and body. Vaccinations may be needed. In most parts of the country, dogs need preventive treatment against parasites such as fleas and ticks. Your vet will probably recommend that you brush your dog's teeth. She will also talk to you about spaying or neutering your dog.

The choice of diets for a dog is staggering. From raw food to premium to commercial, your vet can help you choose what's healthiest for your dog. Most vets can also offer advice or recommend a behaviorist if your dog is acting up. And many offer boarding services. All vets have arrangements for after-hours emergency care. Make sure you know what they are.

V is for Veterinarian

From birth to death there should always be
a veterinarian to oversee
your dog's health from A to Z
so he can live long with vitality.

After thousands of years of crafting specialized breeds, we now have dogs who can serve people in a variety of ways. We're most familiar with assistance dogs, which include guide, hearing, and service dogs. Guide dogs are trained to help sight-impaired people navigate busy city sidewalks and cross busy streets, ride buses, and do other everyday tasks. The first guide dogs were German shepherds. Today nearly any large breed can be trained to do guide dog work as long as the dog is calm, strong, and loves to work.

Hearing dogs are trained to notify their hearing-impaired owners of everyday sounds. They can give an alert to a phone or doorbell ring, a baby's cry, or an alarm. Hearing dogs give their owners a sense of security as well as independence and companionship. Many hearing dogs come from shelters or rescue organizations.

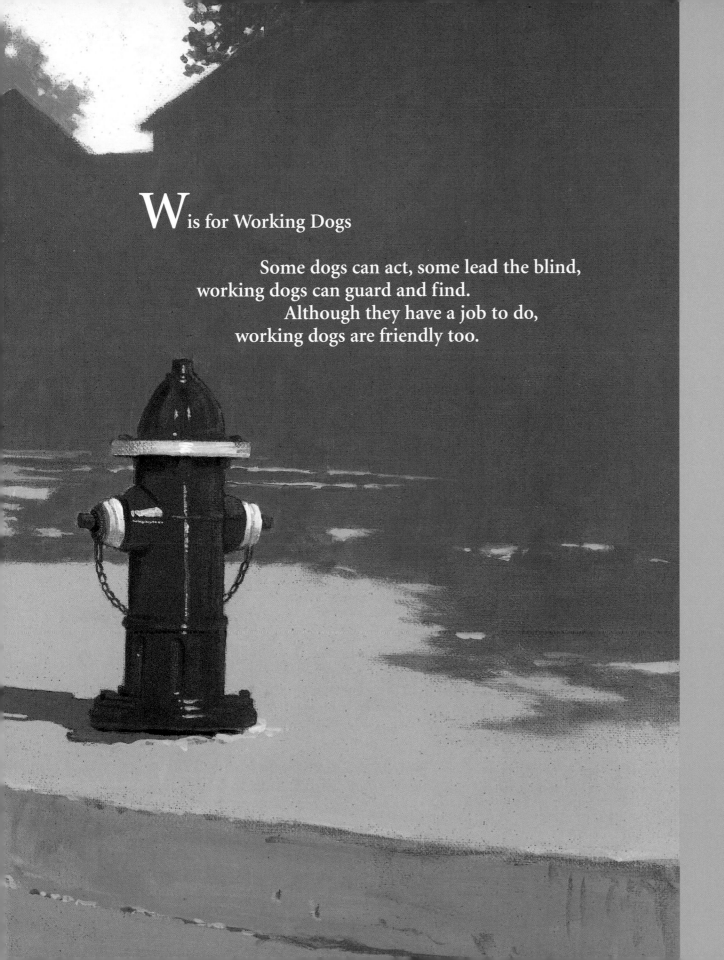

W is for Working Dogs

Some dogs can act, some lead the blind,
working dogs can guard and find.
Although they have a job to do,
working dogs are friendly too.

Service dogs are trained to assist people in wheelchairs and those with other challenges like psychiatric disorders, chronic pain, and seizures. Their skills depend on the needs of their owner. Some are trained to pick up dropped items, turn lights on and off, or push a preprogrammed button on the phone to call for emergency help.

Dogs have been used in wars for four thousand years. They have served as messengers, scouts, and guards. They're used to detect mines, track, attack, and rescue. It wasn't until recently, though, that these four-legged military heroes were recognized for their work. Today, monuments are erected and ceremonies are held to honor their service and bravery.

Detection dogs have a variety of jobs. Some are trained to find specific wild animals (or their signs such as fur and droppings) for research and conservation projects. Some are trained to detect termites in buildings. Some are trained to detect items such as bombs and illegal drugs. Beagle Brigades work for the US government at border crossings and some airports. Their job is to check baggage for fruit and meat—foods from other countries that could carry pests or disease.

Dogs have been entertaining us for centuries. They act in movies and on TV. They even act in plays. In the past, though, dog entertainment included dog fights, bull baiting, and other violent activities. Fighting breeds were developed and are still around. Most of these dogs make loving and obedient pets if they are bred and raised properly. Strict laws protect dogs today, and any form of dog fight is illegal.

There seems to be no end to the type of work dogs can and will do for us. It's hard to imagine what the world would be like without them!

X is for Xolo

The Xolo is an ancient breed,
   a type of dog you rarely see.
      Some other breeds, long-lived or not,
         are also those not seen a lot.

Breeds go in and out of style all the time. One year dalmatians may be popular, the next year rottweilers are all the rage. The popularity of a breed is reflected in its high numbers. Breeds with few members are considered rare.

Some breeds are so little known they hardly hit the average person's radar. For instance, how many people have heard of the Xoloitzcuintli? This breed is three thousand years old and was a favorite among the Mayans and Toltecs. It was a popular breed then but is now rarely seen.

Around 400 dog breeds exist today. Of those 400, over 130 are rare breeds. And new breeds continue to be developed. Not all of them have a name as hard to pronounce as Xoloitzcuintli. Of course, you could always refer to the Xoloitzcuintli by one of its easier names, Xolo or the Mexican hairless.

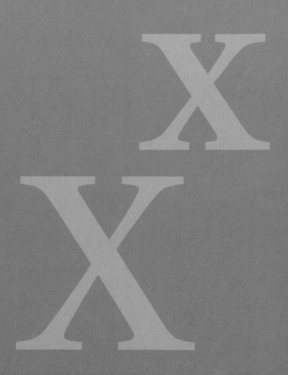

Y is for Yip, Yap, Yelp, Yowl

From the high yap to the low growl,
the whine, the yelp, and even the howl,
dogs seem to have a lot to say
with their voice and their body display.

Woof, woof.

Along with body language, vocalization is an important part of canine communication. The bark is what we think of first when we consider dog "speak." And it is the dog's most used form of vocal expression. Dogs bark when they are bored and excited, as a threat, and as a warning.

The meaning behind a growl can not be mistaken—it's a warning. Dogs growl when they feel fearful, angry, and even irritated. If a growl is ignored, the dog will likely become more aggressive. Watch out!

Whining, although annoying, is another form of communication. Dogs whine to express frustration, fear, and pain. They whine for attention, too. A yelp also expresses pain, and it's the sound a startled dog makes.

The lonely-sounding howl is used in the wild to bring the wolf pack together. Some domestic dogs also howl when left alone. In the wild, howling is a chorus taken up by all the pack members, as it is among many of our neighborhood dogs.

When trying to understand our dogs, it's important to read both their body language and their vocalizations.

A puppy's play is schooling in disguise. Play builds a puppy's coordination and social skills. It teaches a puppy about pack rank and keeps aggression in check. Play-fighting and pretend hunting perfect the grown-up skills. In short, a puppy learns how to be a dog through play.

Older dogs don't give up playtime. They still enjoy romps with other friendly dogs. Play invitations come in the form of the play bow and at times sharp barks. There may be growling and the play may seem rough, but dogs have ways of communicating their friendly intent to each other.

When playing is not enough, puppies and some dogs will suddenly go on a tear. Zigging and zagging around house or yard helps these dogs release built-up energy. When one dog gets a case of the zoomies, other dogs may join in the fun.

Play is important to the development of a dog. Be sure you provide your puppy with plenty of it. You can even join the fun!

Zz

Z is for Zigzag Zoomies

Pent-up energy trapped inside,
    feel it building, there's nowhere to hide.
Playing helps, but after a bit
    zig and zagging is what does the trick.

How old is my dog in human years?

For years people have been multiplying their dog's age by seven to figure out the equivalent age in human years. But small dogs generally live longer than large dogs, so a one-size-fits-all calculation doesn't quite work. A more accurate formula was developed by Fred L. Metzger, DVM, State College, Pennsylvania. Visit his Web site at http://www.metzgeranimal.com/sr1.htm, enter your dog's calendar age and weight, click on Dog, and you'll know how old your dog really is in human years.

Dog Terms

dog fancy: a hobby involving people who are devoted to purebred dogs

earthdog event: a test that measures the skills of dachshunds and small terriers to follow and corner animals who burrow underground

field trial: a competition among dogs that tests hunting skills and performance

flyball: a relay race run by teams of four dogs who sprint over four hurdles, catch a ball from the flyball box, and race back over the hurdles

gun dog: a dog bred to help hunters find or chase the animals they're hunting

hunt test: a test that evaluates how well an individual dog's hunting skills meet the established standard

K-9: a term that is a play on the word *canine,* meaning "dog." The term *K-9* originated in the military and is based on its general staff divisions, G-1, G-2, G-3, G-4, G-5.

Constellations

Throughout history, people of nearly all cultures around the world have seen patterns in the stars, what we call constellations. But not everyone saw the same patterns. In 1929 the International Astronomical Union (IAU) officially identified eighty-eight constellations. We don't get to see them all, though. Those of us who live in the northern hemisphere cannot see the constellations that decorate the sky in the southern hemisphere, and vice versa.

To earn a Canine Good Citizen certificate, a dog must pass ten tests:

1. Accepting a friendly stranger
2. Sitting politely for petting
3. Appearance and grooming
4. Out for a walk (walking on a loose lead)
5. Walking through a crowd
6. Sit and down on command and staying in place
7. Coming when called
8. Reaction to another dog
9. Reaction to distraction
10. Supervised separation

Fun Facts

- The chow chow's tongue isn't pink like other dogs'—it's bluish black!

- The smallest dog breed is the Chihuahua.

- The tallest dog breed is the Irish wolfhound. But individuals of any breed can surprise us. The tallest dog is a Great Dane named Gibson, who is 43 inches tall at the shoulder.

- The heaviest dog breed is the Old English mastiff, which can weigh up to 230 pounds. Some individuals, though, have been reported to be even heavier than that!

- The Guinness World Record for the most tennis balls in a dog's mouth at one time is five.

- The pit bull is not a true breed. Two breeds that are often mistaken for pit bulls are the Staffordshire bull terrier and the bull terrier.

- At one time, pit bulls were known as nursemaid's or nanny dogs because they were so trustworthy around children.

Rare Breeds

The American Kennel Club (AKC) registers 155 different breeds. But many more breeds are recognized by other kennel clubs around the world. Altogether around 400 dog breeds exist today. Many of these breeds are rare. A breed is considered rare when only a few dogs of that breed are alive.

The ten rarest breeds registered by the AKC in 2006:

Foxhounds (English)	Canaan Dogs
Harriers	Skye Terriers
Glen of Imaal Terriers	Sealyham Terriers
Otterhounds	Komondorok
Foxhounds (American)	Finnish Spitz

To answer the needs of rare breed fanciers, the AKC also runs the Foundation Stock Service (FSS) for all purebred breeds that are not accepted for AKC registration. The *Xoloitzcuintli* (show-low-eats-queent-lee) is one of those rare breeds that is FSS registered. The word *Xoloitzcuintli* is derived from the name of the Aztec god Xolotl and the Aztec word for dog, *itzcuintli*. This breed is more commonly known as the Mexican hairless.

The ten most popular breeds registered by the AKC in 2006:

1. Labrador Retriever	6. Dachshund
2. Yorkshire Terrier	7. Boxer
3. German Shepherd Dog	8. Poodle
4. Golden Retriever	9. Shih Tzu
5. Beagle	10. Miniature Schnauzer

Ruth Strother

Ruth Strother has been in the publishing industry for over twenty years. She was the first editor-in-chief of BowTie Press, the book division of BowTie, Inc., publisher of *Dog Fancy* magazine, among others. She is the author of fourteen books for children, including *My Pet Dog*, which was nominated for several prestigious book awards. Ruth was born in New York and spent her childhood in Minneapolis, Minnesota, poring over any dog books she could find. She has worked and volunteered at zoos and humane societies, and was lucky enough to be able to combine her passion for animals with her career. She now lives in Southern California with her husband and daughter, and their two Labs.

Gijsbert van Frankenhuyzen

Gijsbert (Mr. Nick) was born in the Netherlands in 1951. Being one of eight brothers and sisters, there was barely room for a white mouse let alone a dog or a cat. Four years after he graduated from art school, he immigrated to Michigan to be the art director for the *Michigan Natural Resources Magazine*. He vowed that once he settled into a house out in the country he would get the dog he could never have. He did, and he has had a dog (or two or three) ever since. His dogs are portrayed in his Hazel Ridge Farm series: *Kelly of Hazel Ridge*, *Saving Samantha*, and *Adopted by an Owl*, and of course they are in *W is for Woof*. Mr. Nick travels to schools throughout Michigan teaching kids that drawing is fun and simple. Check out his Web site at www.hazelridgefarm.com.